QUINN
THE QUIRKY QUEEN BEE
Making Alliteration Fun for All Types

Written by
Nicky Gaymer-Jones

Illustrated by
Amber Leigh Luecke

Copyright © 2024 Nicky Gaymer-Jones

All rights reserved. No part of this publication may be reproduced, distributed, or transmitted in any form or by any means, including photocopying, recording, or other electronic or mechanical methods, without the prior written permission of the publisher, except in the case of brief quotations embodied in critical reviews and certain other noncommercial uses permitted by copyright law.

For permission requests, write to the publisher, addressed "Attention: Permission for Use" at the following email: Nicholas.Gaymer.Jones@gmail.com

ISBN: 978-1-964411-16-3 (Paperback)

Any references to historical events, real people, or real places are used fictitiously. Names, characters, and places are products of the author's imagination.

Front cover image and book design by Amber Leigh Luecke

Printed in the United States of America

First printing edition 2024

Dedicated to all of the great teachers who believe in their students.

Quinn the quirky queen dances wherever she flies. Quinn, the quirky queen bee of Quarryville, is quite a prize.

In fact, the quirky queen is quiet and very kind. A queen like that is often hidden and is sometimes hard to find.

Every bee in Quarryville respects their quirky queen. From the way she flies to her quality crown, anyone who knows Quinn the quirky queen speaks of her and beams.

The entire town wants the quirky queen's attention. The quirky queen has earned her reputation, and nothing will make Quinn quit her role as the queen bee of her foundation.

The bees of the world know that quirky Quinn, the queen bee of Quarryville, is the best queen there has been. She is quick on her feet and can fly quite a distance, but the quirky queen prefers to stay and be of assistance.

The quirky queen bee of Quarryville is intelligent and strong. The quirky queen knows best, and the other bees agree she would never steer them wrong.

The bees know Quinn isn't perfect because nobody can be, but they love the quirky queen because she does her best to maintain the hive up in the tree.

The quirky queen keeps them busy in the hive. She teaches them how to live, so the kingdom will always thrive.

Every bee in Quarryville loves the queen they have at present. Quinn the quirky queen bee has always made sure every experience is pleasant.

Quinn the quirky queen bee flies around the hive, making sure that all the bees are getting their chores done by five.

Some of the bees would rather play, but Quinn knows if they work together, then they can all have fun at the end of the day.

Quinn makes sure the other bees make their beds, sweep the floors, and clean up their messes. "After all," says Quinn the quirky queen bee, "if our house is clean and tidy, then nobody stresses."

"Besides, once the chores are done, we can dance, and all have fun."

Discover the Wonders of Alliteration: A Complete Collection from A to Z!

Dive into a world of wonder and learning with the "Alliteration Fun for All Types" Complete Collection, where each amusing story is dedicated to a specific letter of the alphabet.

From adventurous ants to zany zebras, these captivating tales are designed to engage and empower readers of all types, including those with dyslexia or other learning differences.

This collection of fun stories weaves rhythm, rhyming, and the magic of alliteration to foster a love of reading and promote inclusivity in storytelling.

Whether you're seeking an educational adventure, or inspiring a new reader, this collection promises to captivate young minds and instill a lifelong love for the magic of words.

To learn more visit Nickysbooks.com

If you enjoyed this book, please leave a review on Amazon and help new readers discover Nicky's books. Thank you.

Made in the USA
Columbia, SC
15 August 2024

40524521R00015